© Copyright 2014

Written by Sally A Jones and Amanda C Jones
Illustrations by Annalisa C Jones

Published by GUINEA PIG EDUCATION

2 Cobs Way,
New Haw,
Addlestone,
Surrey,
KT15 3AF.
www.guineapigeducation.co.uk

NO part of this publication may be reproduced, stored or copied for commercial purposes and profit without the prior written permission of the publishers.

ISBN: 978-1-907733-85-7

Dear Kids and Parents,

This book contains a structured course to teach children to spell using phonics.

A friendly character, an alien called Zoggy, encourages your child to choose good words for their own writing. In a series of short stories, he teaches the child: to recognise boring over used words, replacing them with interesting vocabulary; to use the right word in the right place; and to substitute easier words for harder ones.

Each challenge includes a vocabulary building exercise with suggested answers. There are also a series of matching exercises to introduce more advanced vocabulary to your child - essential for gaining the higher levels.

Zoggy's guide to a <u>**BREAK**</u> <u>**THROUGH**</u> in VOCABULARY.

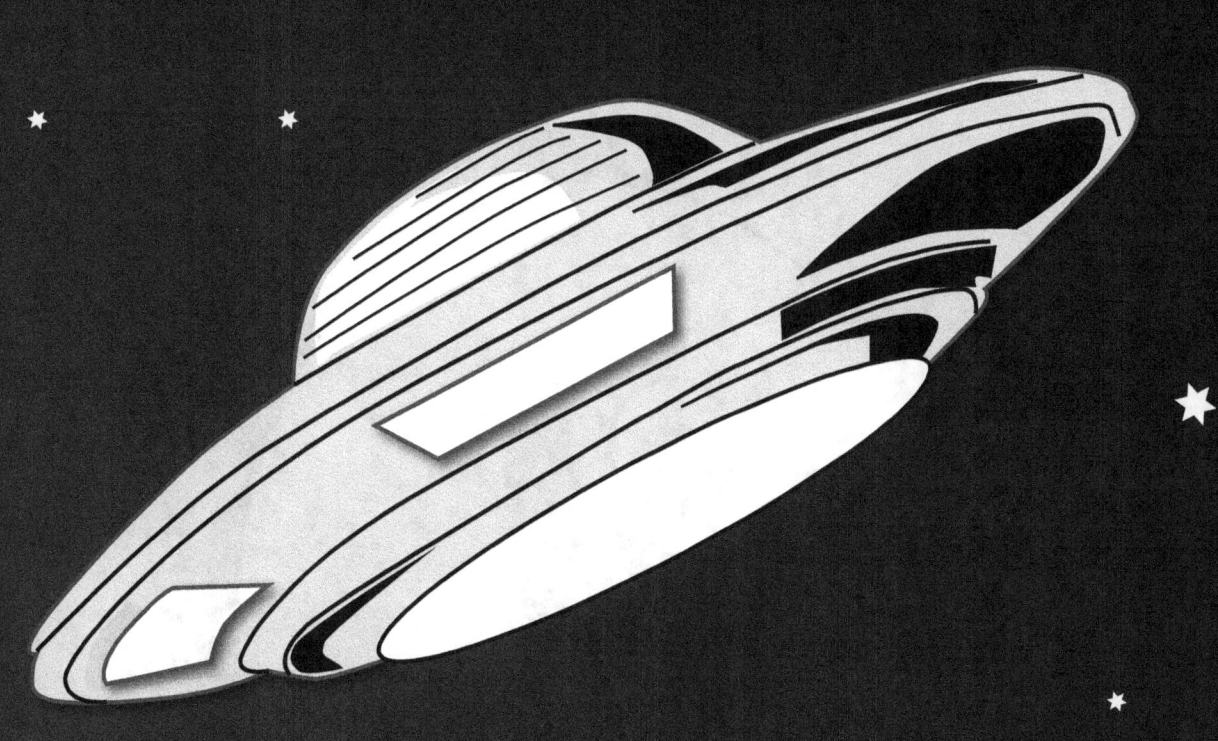

ZOGGI has been sent from planet ZEN, three million light years away.

Shall I tell you what to do?

Yes, I will *ADVISE, GUIDE, RECOMMEND, URGE* you to use some good words.

Am I a **nice** guy?

No, I am a CHEERFUL, JOLLY, HAPPY, LIGHT HEARTED, LIVELY, LIKEABLE and BRILLIANT guy.

Is this a **nice** spaceship?

It's the latest model.

Yes, It's:

| BRIGHT | GLEAMING | VIVID |
| GLOWING | DAZZLING | LUMINOUS |

Am I <u>GOOD</u> at my work?

Yes, I'm <u>SMART</u>.

This is my report from Zen:

ZEN PRIMARY SCHOOL

KEEN	TO READ
ABLE	TO WRITE STORIES, RECORDS EXCELLENT DETAILS IN HIS NOTEBOOK.
IMPECCABLE	SPELLING
PERCEPTIVE	IN PROBLEM SOLVING
ASTUTE	AT MATHS
SHREWD UNDERSTANDING	OF ALL SUBJECTS
OUTSTANDING	ART WORK

TEACHERS COMMENT:

ZOGGY IS AN ALERT, CLEVER, INTELLIGENT, SMART, BRIGHT, BRAINY, PERCEPTIVE ALIEN.

WELL DONE!

I always **achieve** top marks in tests.

I **complete** all my homework.

I **perform** well in all subjects.

I **accomplish** all my targets.

Am I **good** at doing all the things earth people do?

I am **COMPETENT** to fly my space vehicle, because I passed my test.

I am **CAPABLE** and **INTELLIGENT** to make the journey from Zen to earth.

It takes **GREAT SKILL** to manoeuvre a space craft through space.

But... I am a **PROFICIENT** space explorer.

TASK
Write an introductory paragraph *introducing* Zoggy, using more **ADVANCED vocabulary**.

TIME FOR A TEST:

Zoggy says, "I have picked out some earth words. Match them to their meanings."

disappoint	fair
shock	to become less active
relax	haughty
praise	bent
proud	trick
intelligent	comfort or calm
illustration	**to make sad**
honest	direct or guide
crooked	fast or sudden
cheat	a sudden, violent force
soothe	where plays are performed
steer	ability to learn
style	to speak well of
swift	an amount
theatre	way of doing something
supply	picture to go with words
thermometer	not knowing what is going on
vinegar	an instrument for measuring
unconscious	method or organised scheme
system	sour liquid

The search for a holiday home

He visits the estate agent who writes down his requirements.

> "I am looking for a **nice** house near a spacecraft launch pad. I want a **nice** garden surrounding the property with many **nice** earth flowers and **nice** fruit trees, which is big enough to set up a satellite, so I can communicate with friends and family on the other side of the universe on Planet Zen.
>
> I need a **nice** loft with a **nice** view of the sky from the window, that is suitable to position my telescope. A **nice** garage is also required to store my spacecraft, so it is out of view and doesn't attract too much attention.
>
> Finally, the property must be **nice**. It must have **nice** bedrooms to entertain alien guests from Planet Zen. It will need **nice** cupboards to store space equipment and specimens collected on earth."

How about this one?

Zoggy grumbles, **"THIS HOUSE IS NOT INTERESTING AT ALL."**

TASK

Can you make the description more interesting?

Replace the word 'nice' with other adjectives.

The following pages will teach you the importance of using the right word in the right place.

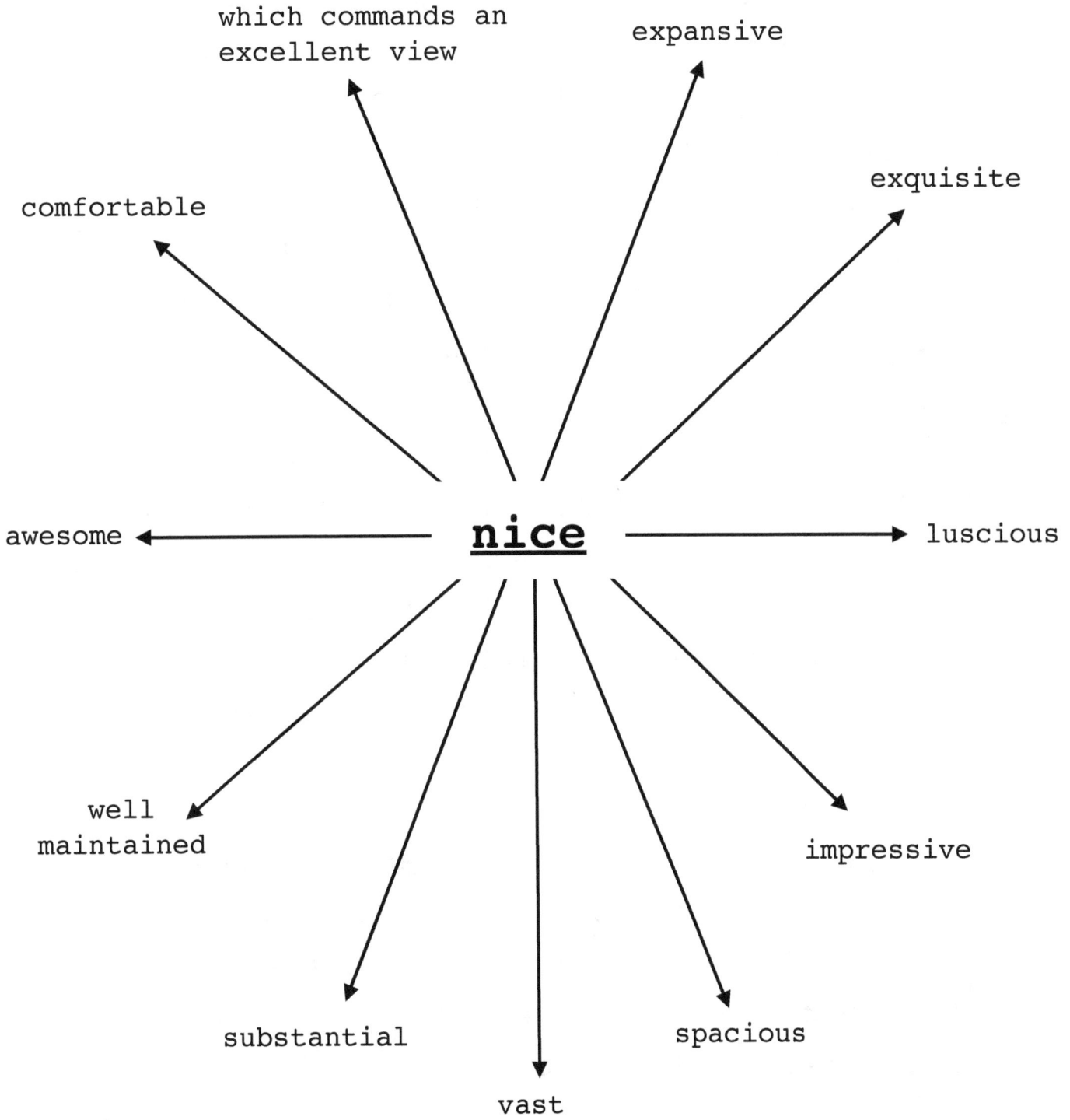

TIP

e.g. *a ~~nice~~ room* could become ***a <u>comfortable</u> room***

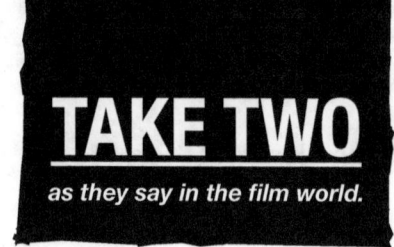

"I am looking for an **impressive** house near a spacecraft launch pad. I want an **awesome** garden surrounding the property with **exquisite** earth flowers and **luscious** fruit trees, which is big enough to set up a satellite, so I can communicate with friends and family on the other side of the universe on Planet Zen.

I need an **expansive** loft which **commands an excellent** view of the sky from the window, that is suitable to position my telescope. A **substantial** garage is also required to store my spacecraft, so it is out of view and doesn't attract too much attention.

Finally, the property must be **well maintained**. It must have **spacious** and **comfortable** bedrooms to entertain alien guests from Planet Zen. It will need **vast** cupboards to store space equipment and specimens collected on earth."

THIS HOUSE SOUNDS GREAT!

TIME FOR A TEST:

> Zoggy says, "I have picked out some earth words. Match them to their meanings."

meteorite	something that is owned
parliament	A flat bony sea fish
receipt	**a piece of matter from earth**
reflect	something given or sent to you
microscope	to feel or show great joy
research	an instrument that makes small objects look large.
unconscious	to know someone again
plaice	the study of a subject, so as to learn some new facts.
rejoice	not knowing what is going on around you and not feeling anything.
receive	a note saying something has been paid for
property	the group of people who make the laws of the country
recognise	to throw back light, heat, sound or picture.

Zoggy's Earth Home

It has **got** several spacious rooms. One has **got** a bed to lie on; another has **got** a comfortable sofa, a table and some chairs.

The house has **got** heat coming from metal grids on the wall and it has **got** water in those metal objects that you turn on (called 'taps' by earthlings).

Besides this, the house has **got** some very primitive devices; a phone and a wifi internet system, so the earthlings can communicate across the world and send each other messages.

Zoggy shakes his head in disbelief. He thinks that there is much he could teach earthlings.

The house has not **got** any robots to do the housework, though it has got a fridge, a washing machine, a freezer, a microwave oven – which looks a bit rusty. He is not sure how to use them.

It has not **got** the intergalactic computer system 'Solar Net' to communicate with all worlds across the universes and in the depths of space.

"Annoying! I feel cut off," Zoggy grumbles.

TASK

These 'got' words make my earth holiday home sound so boring. Rewrite the passage putting in better words for 'got.'

Remember, it is important to use the right word in the right place.

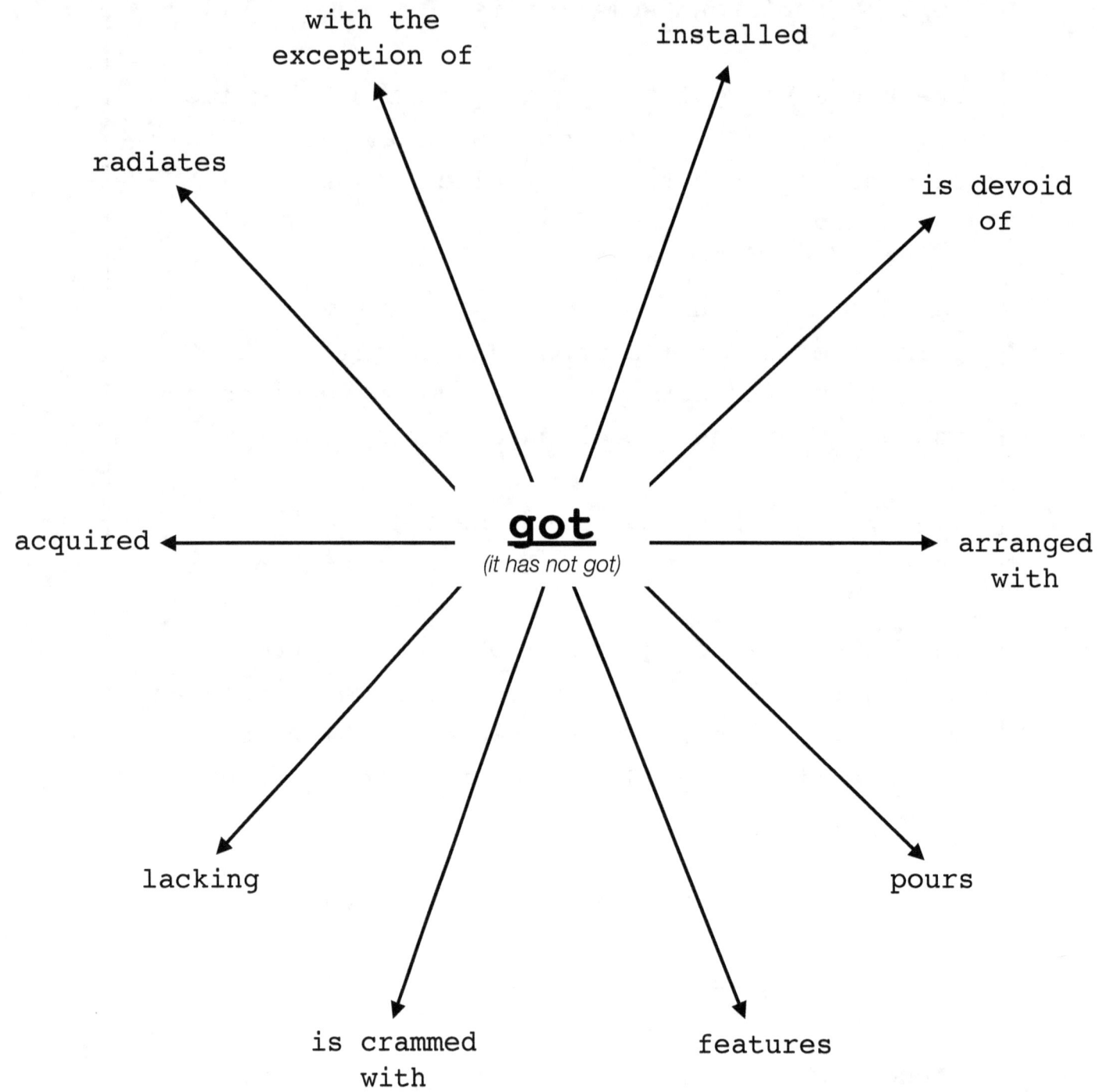

TIP

e.g. ***it has ~~got~~*** could become ***it <u>features</u>***

Fill in the gaps with more advanced vocabulary. Use the words and phrases on the previous page to help you.

My house .... several spacious rooms. In one room a big bed has been .... to lie down on, while another is .... a luxurious sofa, a table and some chairs.

The house .... heat that comes from metal grids on the wall and water .... from the taps.

Besides this, the house .... some very primitive devices; a phone and a wifi internet system, which enables the occupant to receive and transmit messages across the globe and also providing satellite TV.

Zoggy shakes his head in disbelief. He concludes that there is much he could teach earthlings.

The house .... any robots to do the housework, ... a fridge, a washing machine, a freezer and a hazardous looking microwave oven. He is not sure how to use these devices.

It has not .... the latest intergalactic computer system 'Solar net', to communicate with worlds deep into outer space.

"Annoying! I feel isolated from my own lands," Zoggy says.

Check your answers.

My house **features** several spacious rooms. In one room a big bed has been **installed** to lie down on, while another is **arranged with** a luxurious sofa, a table and some chairs.

The house **radiates** heat that comes from metal grids on the wall and water **pours** from the taps.

Besides this, the house **is crammed with** some very primitive devices; a phone and a wifi internet system, which enables the occupant to receive and transmit messages across the globe and also providing satellite TV.

Zoggy shakes his head in disbelief. He concludes that there is much he could teach earthlings.

The house **is devoid of/lacking** any robots to do the housework, **with the exception of** a fridge, a washing machine, a freezer and a hazardous looking microwave oven. He is not sure how to use these devices.

It has not **acquired** the latest intergalactic computer system 'Solar net', to communicate with worlds deep into outer space.

"Annoying! I feel isolated from my own lands," Zoggy grumbles.

Zoggy sets to work, using his Zen computer, to download some helpful home improvements, to equip his earth home with some hi-tech gadgets and intergalactic space devices like they use on Zen.

First, he equips his earth house with robots to do all the work, serve him and bring him tea. What other tasks will the robots do? What other devices does Zoggy download?

For example:

- *An automatic door-opening device. A device that senses you coming and opens the door automatically.*

-

-

-

REPLACE that bossy word 'GET.'

GET TO	GET BACK	GET UP
arrive	recover	arise
come	repossess	rise
reach	regain	stand
land at	recuperate	wake up
touch down at	reclaim	awaken

GET BY	GET ROUND	GET HOLD OF
exist	persuade	achieve
manage	win over	attain
get along	convince	obtain
cope	sway	acquire

GET OUT	GET IT	(continued)
escape	fathom	find
evade	understand	search out
dodge	latch on	dig up
retreat	comprehend	come into possession of
evacuate	grasp	fetch
break out	see	hunt
		secure

GET OVER	GET OFF/DOWN	GET TOGETHER
survive	alight	congregate
live through	descend	gather
recover from	dismount	meet
		assemble
		gather

Read through the words on the previous page. Cover and write.
How many can you remember?

GET TO	**GET BACK**	**GET UP**
....	....	....
....	....	....
....	....	....
....	....	....
....	....	....

GET BY	**GET ROUND**	**GET HOLD OF**
....	....	....
....	....	....
....	....	....
....	....	....

GET OUT	**GET IT**	
....	....	....
....	....	....
....	....	....
....	....	....
....	....	....
....	....	....

GET OVER	**GET OFF/DOWN**	**GET TOGETHER**
....	....	....
....	....	....
....	....	....
		....
		....

First Visitor

A hungry creature **looks** out of the hole. The **noise** of snores **tells** him that Zoggy must be **fast** asleep in his chair. The **leftover** lunch **is** on the kitchen table and he **wants** to **eat** the **nice scraps of food**. The alien **opens** a sleepy eye. He stretches, yawns and stands up. He **seems to know** something is there.

The alien **begins** to look round the room, but it is too late because the little mouse **goes** to safety. Zoggy **goes back** to sleep in his **warm** chair.

BORING!

Zoggy says, "Rewrite this passage to make it more interesting by using different words. Replace the underlined words with new words which have similar meanings."

Fill in the gaps with more advanced vocabulary. Use the words and phrases below to help you.

encountered	peers	retreats	nibble
conducts	proceeds	weird	remnants
grabs	raises	deeply	conscious of
informs	lay	stretches	investigation
scurries	sound	cosy	scrumptious morsels

The hungry mouse .... out of the hole. The .... of snores .... him that Zoggy is .... asleep in his chair. The .... of his lunch .... on the kitchen table and he .... to .... the .... The alien .... a sleepy eye. He ...., yawns and stands up. He is ... a strange presence.

Is it a .... earth phenomenon he has never .... before? He .... his notebook to record his findings.

He .... a thorough ...., but it is too late because the little mouse .... to safety. Zoggy .... to his .... chair.

TAKE TWO

Check your answers

A hungry creature **peers** out of the hole. The **sound** of snores **informs** him that Zoggy is **deeply** asleep in his chair. The **remains** of his lunch **lay** on the kitchen table and he **proceeds** to **nibble** the **scrumptious morsels**. The alien **raises** a sleepy eye. He **stretches**, yawns and stands up. He is **conscious of** a strange presence.

Is it a **weird** earth phenomenon he has never **encountered** before? He **grabs** his notebook to record his findings.

He **conducts** a thorough **investigation**, but it is too late because the little mouse **scurries** to safety. Zoggy **retreats** to his **cosy** chair.

TIME FOR A TEST:

Zoggy says, "I have picked out some earth words. Match them to their synonyms (words that have the same meanings."

talent	**immense**
massive	**bold**
admire	**portion**
delicate	**ability**
dependable	**kind**
adventurous	**agreeable**
catastrophic	**respect**
beg	**colossal**
benevolent	**fragile**
delightful	**scrounge**
chunk	**loyal**
huge	**fatal**
mighty	**powerful**
despicable	**hateful**

Last week the neighbours met Zoggy.

"An alien, did you say an alien?" **said** Dan.

"Yes! He's moved in to number 7," **said** Jack.

"Hope he won't create a disturbance," **said** Dan.

"This has always been a quiet road."

"That's right," **said** Jack.

"Perhaps we should pop in and introduce ourselves," **said** Jack.

"Good idea," **said** Dan.

The neighbours knock on the door.

"Coming," **said** Zoggy. "I'm coming. Just got to finish my live report on 'Sky Time' to Zen."

"Sounds a bit ..." **said** Dan quietly to his friend.

"Touchy..." **said** Jack.

"Greetings from Zen," **said** Zoggy, throwing the door wide open and shaking their hands firmly, as he has seen earth people do.

"Good to meet you," **said** Dan nervously.

"Do step inside," **said** Zoggy. "Excuse the chaos. I've not finished sorting things out," he said.

"Are you sure you don't mind?" **said** Dan, walking in.

"Amazing place! You have a lot of technology," **said** Jack.

"I need it to communicate with my family in Zen."

"I hear you come from outer space."

"Yes a universe 10 million light years from here."

"How long does it take you to get back?" **said** Dan.

"No more than an hour," **said** Zoggy, "with my top of the range zennel space craft."

"Wow! Awesome!" **said** Dan and Jack in amazement.

"By the way," **said** Jack, "just a word of warning, the residents committee doesn't like space craft parked in the street."

"I'll try and keep it in the garage," **said** Zoggy.

"Noisy parties don't go down well either," **said** Jack.

"When I have visitors, I'll put on silent mode," **said** Zoggy smiling.

The neighbours exchanged glances.

Zoggy says, "My neighbours sound quite dull. Let's make them more interesting by taking out 'said' and replacing it with better words."

Remember, it is important to use the right word in the right place.

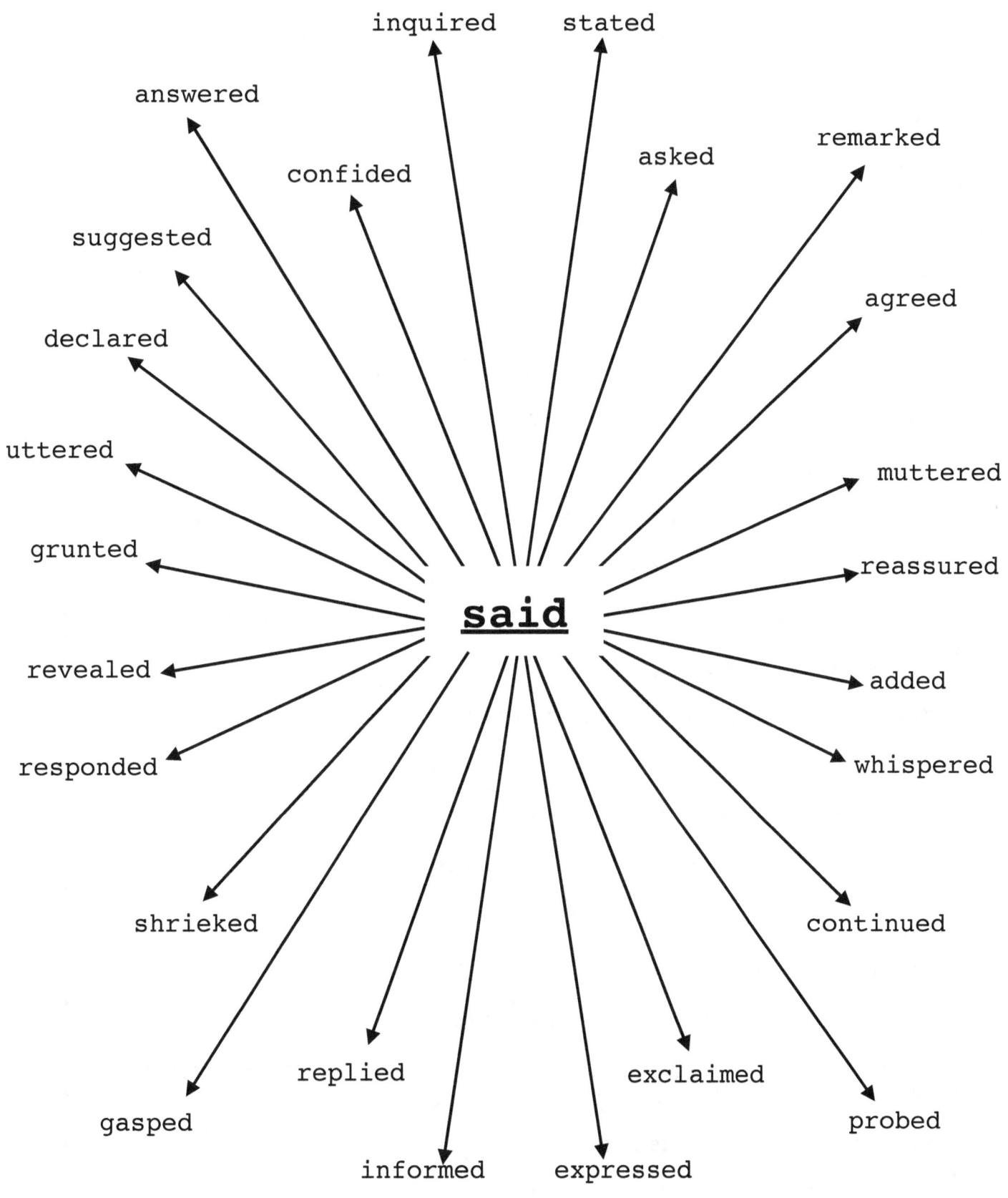

TIP

e.g. *he ~~said~~* could become **he <u>exclaimed</u> loudly**

TAKE TWO

"An alien, did you say an alien?" **asked** Dan.

"Yes! He's moved into number 7," **replied** Jack.

"Hope he won't create a disturbance," **added** Dan. "This has always been a quiet road."

"That's right," **grunted** Jack. "Perhaps we should pop in and introduce ourselves," **suggested** Jack.

"Good idea," **agreed** Dan.

The neighbours knock on the door.

"Coming," **shrieked** Zoggy. "I'm coming. Just going to finish my live report on 'Sky Time' to Zen."

"Sounds a bit ..." **confided** Dan quietly to his friend.

"Touchy..." **continued** Jack.

"Greetings from Zen," **exclaimed** Zoggy, throwing the door wide open and shaking their hands firmly.

"Good to meet you," **uttered** Dan nervously.

"Do step inside," **muttered** Zoggy, "excuse the chaos. I've not finished sorting things out," he **whispered**.

"Are you sure you don't mind?" **responded** Dan, walking in.

"Amazing place! You have a lot of technology, **gasped** Jack.

"I need it to communicate with my family in Zen," the alien **remarked**.

"I hear you come from outer space," he **probed** gently.

"Yes a universe 10 million light years from here," he **answered**.

"How long does it take you to get back?" **inquired** Dan.

"No more than an hour," **stated** Zoggy, with my top of the range zennel space craft."

"Wow! Awesome!" **expressed** Dan and Jack in amazement.

"By the way," **informed** Jack, "just a word of warning, the residents committee doesn't like space craft parked in the street."

"I'll try and keep it in the garage," **reassured** Zoggy.

"Noisy parties don't go down well either," **revealed** Jack.

"When I have visitors, I'll put on silent mode," **declared** Zoggy smiling.

The neighbours exchange glances.

TIME FOR A TEST:

> Zoggy says, "I have picked out some earth words. Match them to their synonyms (words that have the same meanings."

solemn	**cheer**
faith	**sure**
occur	**serious**
instruct	**bold**
just	**burst**
fresh	**comfort**
fix	**well known**
connect	**belief**
ancient	**happen**
collect	**fair**
certain	**confuse**
brave	**praise**
compliment	**new**
calm	**fight**
mix up	**teach**
admit	**fasten**
famous	**old**
encourage	**gather**
explode	**confess**
soothe	**join**
wrestle	**peaceful**

Zoggy takes a walk.

It is a beautiful day for a **walk** in the park. Zoggy, the alien from Planet Zen, **walks** over the freshly mown grass and **walks** slowly past the clusters of fragrant purple flowers. He sniffs the air. What joy!

Then, he **walks** towards the sparkling lake, **walks** on to the muddy beach and **walks** his metal toes in the cool, soothing ripples. Ducks and geese **walk** through the marshy grasses around him.

A few minutes later, he **walks** towards the overgrown path and **walks** through the roots of the straggling plants. Suddenly, he **trips** and topples over.

A curious rat **walks** round his feet, a shy water vole softly **walks** by and the squirrel **runs** madly up a tree. Zoggy manages to **walk** over to the bench, where a shaggy dog **walks** up to him with his tongue lolling out. This is too much for Zoggy, the alien, so he **walks off** like a wounded soldier in the direction of home.

What an idyllic scene, but it sounds like a BORING walk with all those 'walk' words.

Let us replace them with more **ADVANCED VOCABULARY**.

stroll	waddle	marches off
saunters	immerses	tiptoes through
staggers	totters	races over to
tramples over	stumbles	slinks off
ambles	darts	continues
hobbles	approaches	dashes
descends to	strides towards	paddles
scampers	bounds	wanders
scurries	clambers	advances

Can you think of any more?

Remember to think about the context of a word.

Walk can mean stroll, amble, walk towards or approach.

Walk down can mean descend.

Walk up can mean ascend.

TAKE TWO

It is a beautiful day for a **stroll** in the park. Zoggy, the alien from Planet Zen, **tramples over** the freshly mown grass and **ambles** slowly past the clusters of fragrant purple flowers. He sniffs the air. What joy!

Then, he **approaches** the sparkling lake, **continues** on to the muddy beach and **immerses** his metal toes in the cool, soothing ripples. Ducks and geese **waddle** through the marshy grasses around him.

A few minutes later, he **saunters** towards the overgrown path and **clambers through** the roots of the straggling plants. Suddenly, he **stumbles** and topples over.

A curious rat **scurries** round his feet, a shy water vole softly **scampers** by and a squirrel **darts** madly up a tree. Zoggy manages to **hobble** over to the bench, where a shaggy dog **bounds** up to him with his tongue lolling out. This is too much for Zoggy, the alien, so he **slinks off** like a wounded solider in the direction of home.

Read, cover and write your own version.

TIME FOR A TEST:

> Zoggy says, "I have picked out some earth words. Show that you know their meaning by writing each one in a sentence. You can use a dictionary to help you."

WORD	MEANING
neglected	
disbelief	
encounter	
restore	
cautiously	
silhouette	
restore	
concede	
indicate	
reluctant	
defend	
forlorn	
install	
occupant	
react	
disentangle	
conceal	
survivor	
confide	
evidence	
absent mindedly	

Zoggy is spying on earth – as he collects data to take back to Zen.

CAN YOU **SEE** HIM?

PERCEIVE   *LOOK*   *NOTICE*   *OBSERVE*

SIGHT   *GLIMPSE*   *SPOT*   *DETECT*

WHERE IS HE?

"How many better words for 'see' can you think of?" asks Zoggy.

Zoggy spies a school. He <u>sees</u> that learning is "easy-peasy".

Zoggy <u>sees</u> a sign pointing to a school. He <u>sees</u> that earth people <u>see</u> learning to be important and <u>sees</u> that children need to go to school.

He spies on an earth school at work. What can Zoggy <u>learn</u> to take back to Zen?

In science, he <u>learns</u> some important scientific facts about earth. In maths, he <u>learns</u> some essential formulas. In English, he <u>sees</u> some people need a bit of Zoggy help with spelling, grammar and punctuation, but he <u>sees</u> there are some great novels to be read in English literature.

Then, in the afternoon, he <u>sees</u> that painting in art is very relaxing, he <u>sees</u> that P.E. will improve his physical fitness while, in geography, he <u>sees</u> that he will be able to collect some useful information about Earth.

In history, he does not <u>see</u> how he will ever remember all those facts.

Worse than this, he <u>sees</u> that I.T. is much too easy. The computer systems are so out of date.

HE IS SHOCKED! EARTHLINGS HAVE MUCH TO LEARN FROM ZEN!

Remember, it is important to use the right word in the right place.

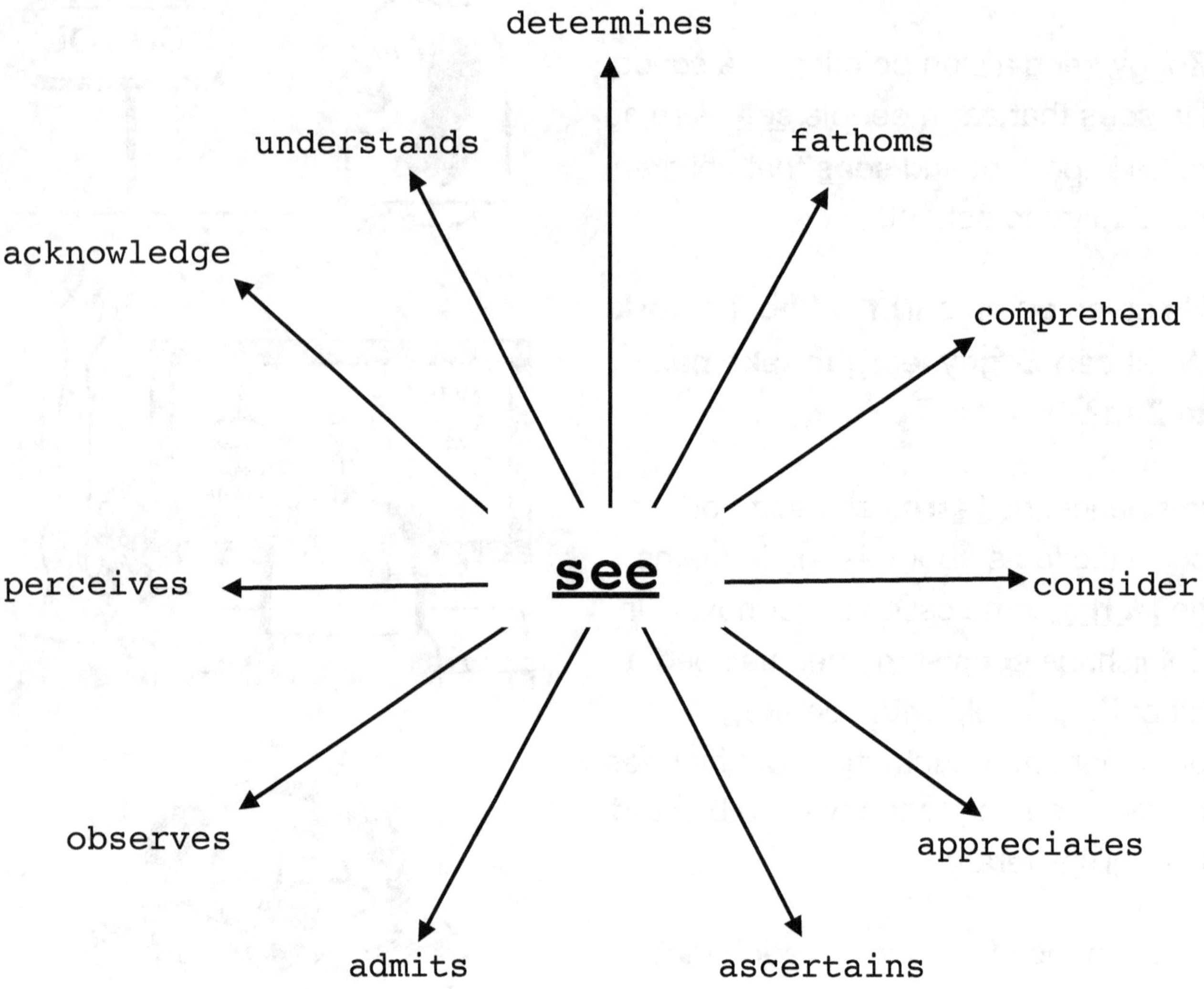

see

- determines
- understands
- fathoms
- acknowledge
- comprehend
- perceives
- consider
- observes
- appreciates
- admits
- ascertains

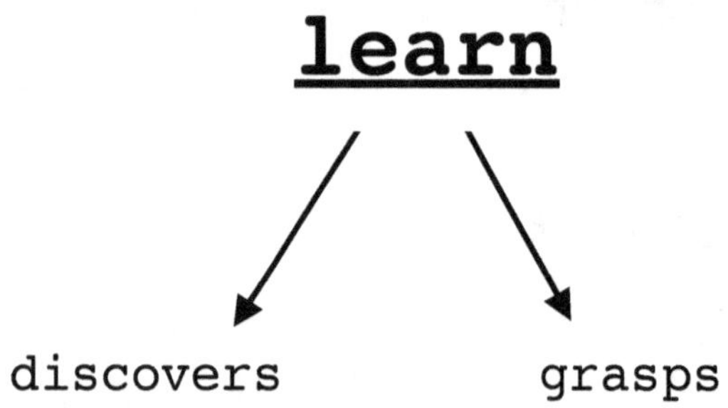

learn

- discovers
- grasps

TIP

e.g. *he* ~~sees~~ could become ***he observes***

TAKE TWO

"The school sounds very dull," exclaims Zoggy, "with all those 'see' and 'learn' words. Rewrite the passage to make it more interesting."

Zoggy **observes** a sign pointing to a school.

He **fathoms** that earth people **consider** learning to be important and he **understands** why children go to school.

He spies on an earth school at work.

In science, he **discovers** some important scientific facts about earth. In maths he **grasps** some essential formulas. In English he **ascertains** that there are some earth people who need a bit of Zoggy help with spelling, grammar and punctuation, but he **acknowledges** that there are some great novels to be read in English literature.

Then, in the afternoon, he **appreciates** that painting in art is very relaxing, he **admits** that P.E. will improve his physical fitness while, in geography, he **determines** that he will be able to collect some useful information about earth.

In history, he fails to **comprehend** how he will ever remember all those facts.

Worse than this, he **perceives** that I.T. is much too easy. He is shocked by the out of date computer systems. Earthlings have much to learn from Planet Zen.

Read, cover and write your own version.

Zoggy exclaims, "Let's learn some **even harder** verbs."

discuss	evade	comprehend
confide	strive	imagine
amend	respect	dispense
reveal	impart	

SHALL I EXTERMINATE THESE WORDS?   NO!

Let's find out what they mean.

Let's match each harder verb to a group of words with a similar meaning. Can you add other words?

---

fathom
perceive
understand
grasp

is the same as

com............

---

alter
change
improve
modify

is the same as

am............

---

communicate
make known
confide
disclose

is the same as

im............

---

conceive
devise
envisage
conjure up

means

ima............

---

deal out
allocate
allot
distribute

means

dis............

---

debate
deliberate
consult with
exchange views

means

disc............

---

avoid
escape
get away from
dodge

means

ev............

---

admit to
divulge
confess
disclose

means

con............

---

attempt
endeavour to
exert oneself
to do all one can

means

str............

---

give away   make known   show   uncover

means

rev............

---

esteem   honour   value

means

res............

Zoggy spies on the places earth people visit.

Zoggy **goes** to the leisure complex. He **goes up** the escalator to the shopping mall and then **goes down**. He **goes up and down** several times. This is cool he thinks.

When he gets bored, he **goes** into a fashion store, but there are no designer outfits that fit an alien.

After this, he **goes** to the 3D multi screen cinema, but the glasses do not fit his alien eyes. Rubbish he mutters to himself!

He **goes** on a trip to the kids play zone. First, he **goes** up the rock face, he **goes** on the trampoline and **goes** round the roller-skating course.

Next, he **goes** outside to survey the assault course. He swings on the tyre, although his alien arms and legs are not made for human activities. His body is too metallic. How frustrating!

What can an alien do on earth?

Finally, he **goes** back to the library and sits at a computer.

He is most definitely back in his comfort zone.

Remember, it is important to use the right word in the right place.

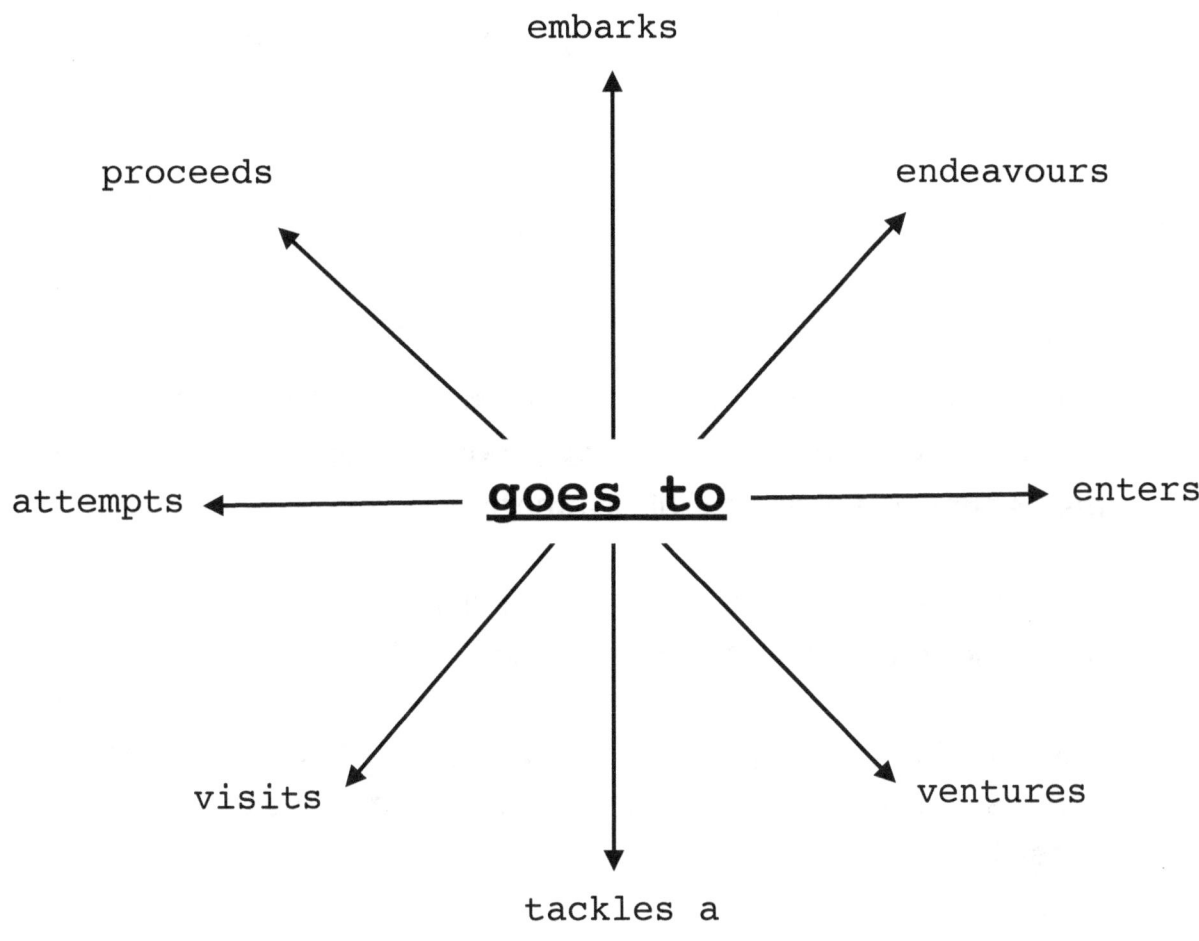

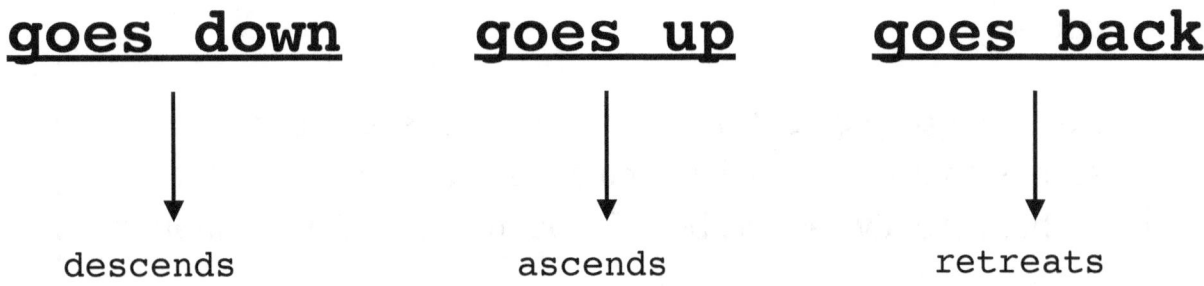

TIP

    e.g. *he ~~goes to~~* could become *he **<u>attempts to</u>***

TAKE TWO

> Zoggy exclaims, "The leisure complex is so, so, so boring with so many words like 'goes'. Rewrite the passage replacing the underlined words with more interesting vocabulary."

Zoggy **visits** the leisure complex. He **ascends** the escalator to the shopping mall and then **descends**. He **ascends and descends** several times. This is amazing he thinks.

When he gets bored, he **enters** into a fashion store, but there are no designer outfits that suit an alien.

After this, he **proceeds** to the 3D multi screen cinema, but the glasses do not fit his alien eyes. Rubbish he mutters to himself!

He **embarks** on a trip to the kids play zone. First, he **attempts** to climb the rock face, he **endeavours** to keep his balance on the trampoline and **tackles a** roller-skating course.

Next, he **ventures** outside to survey the assault course. He swings on the tyre, but his alien arms and legs are not cut out for human activities. His body is too metallic. How frustrating!

What can an alien do on earth?

Finally, he **retreats** to the library and sits at a computer.

Read, cover and write your own version.

Remember words have DIFFERENT MEANINGS

For each new word the most common dictionary definitions have been given.

However, when you look up the meaning of an unfamiliar word, you must decide which definition in the dictionary is the right one to fit the context of the passage you are reading

Some adjectives sound right with a particular noun. Match these adjectives to the most suitable noun.

Exercise 1

modern	suspicion
complete	expression
grim	mountain
prize	message
beautiful	technology
strong	furniture
sinister	possession
distant	surprise
valuable	scenery
antique	treasure

Exercise 2

savage	cardboard
stern	joke
bloodthirsty	teacher
serious	performance
hilarious	measures
luscious	evidence
incompetent	monster
outstanding	warrior
flimsy	fruit
insufficient	consideration

ANSWERS *Did you get them right?*

EXERCISE 1

modern	technology
complete	surprise
grim	expression
prize	possession
beautiful	scenery
strong	suspicion
sinister	message
distant	mountain
valuable	treasure
antique	furniture

EXERCISE 2

savage	warrior
stern	measures
bloodthirsty	monster
serious	consideration
hilarious	joke
luscious	fruit
incompetent	teacher
outstanding	performance
flimsy	cardboard
insufficient	evidence

Zoggy spies on a popular restaurant in town.

First he *eats* an earth meal.

For the starter he *eats* ....

For the main course he *eats* ....

For the dessert he *eats* ....

Write these sentences replacing the word 'eats' with a better word like:

chooses	selects	orders
asks for	demands	opts for

The diners in the restaurant pretend to ignore Zoggy. Why?

Does he have table manners?

Entering the restaurant, he asks for a table; the waiter shows him to his place and he sits down. Zoggy looks at the menu and orders some nice human food.

Zoggy **eats** his starter cautiously, which consists of lobster and crab garnished with salad leaves.

Next, he **eats** his main course, which comprises of a lamb chop and steamed vegetables.

After this, he **eats** his dessert greedily, like a hungry wolf - consisting of fresh pineapple slices and Cornish ice cream.

Zoggy **eats** heartily, but he does not **eat** like a human, preferring to **eat** food in one gulp.

Next, he **leans back** in his chair, sighs and rubs his tummy because he is **feeling rather full**.

Mimicking the other diners, Zoggy **waves over** the waiter to **ask** for the bill. Immediately, the waiter **comes over** with the chip and pin machine.

Oh no! Zoggy has no bank card. Will he be made to do the washing up?

The waiter **eyes** the carpet in **horror** because **most of** the food is on the floor.

Can you finish the story?

> Zoggy exclaims, "The restaurant sounds quite dull. Let's make it more interesting by taking out 'eat' and other boring words and replacing them with better words."

You can also note down some of the other good words used in the passage e.g. *reclines, summons, demands, approaches, observes*.

devours	gobbles	nibbles
chew	swallow	consumes
wolfs down	munches	snacks
guzzles	gulps	gorges
overindulges	overeats	stuffs himself
crunches	chomps	puts away
gets through	scoffs	swigs
bolts down		

TAKE TWO

Read, cover and write your own version.

Entering the restaurant, he asks for a table; the waiter shows him to his place and he sits down. Zoggy **peruses** the menu and orders some **mouth watering** human food.

Zoggy **nibbles** his starter cautiously, which consists of lobster and crab garnished with salad leaves.

Next, he **munches** his main course, which comprises of a lamb chop and steamed vegetables.

After this, he **devours** his dessert greedily, like a hungry wolf - composed of fresh pineapple slices and Cornish ice cream

Zoggy **consumes** his food heartily, but he does not **chew** up his food like humans, preferring to **swallow** it in one gulp.

He **reclines** in his chair, sighs and rubs his tummy because he has **overindulged**.

Mimicking the other diners, Zoggy **summons** the waiter to **demand** the bill. Immediately, the waiter **approaches** with the chip and pin machine.

Oh no! Zoggy has no bankcard. Will he be made to do the washing up?

The waiter **observes** the carpet in **dismay** because **the majority** of the food is on the floor.

Be careful Zoggy you will get *overweight*, **obese**, plump, **tubby**, podgy, plump, *rounded* and **fat** if you overindulge that much!

What did you think of the earth menu Zoggy?

Write a review to show what Zoggy thought, in a few paragraphs.

YUM!

AMAZING	DELICIOUS	YUMMY
DELECTABLE	SCRUMPTIOUS	APPETIZING
TASTY	MOUTH WATERING	DELIGHTFUL

YUK!

GHASTLY	DISGUSTING	REVOLTING
BAD	HORRIBLE	REPULSIVE
SICKENING	AWFUL	DREADFUL
HORRID	UNSPEAKABLE	ATROCIOUS

Match the adjectives to the most suitable noun.

EXERCISE 3

torrential	teenager
shrewd	mind
elderly	expression
sprightly	old man
chaotic	neighbourhood
inquiring	rain
lavish	mess
sulky	person
affluent	politician
solemn	lifestyle

EXERCISE 4

aggressive	identity
candid	warning
impressive	coincidence
official	home
cultural	dressing
amazing	indignation
righteous	behaviour
sterile	words
harsh	opinion

ANSWERS *Did you get them right?*

EXERCISE 3

torrential	rain
shrewd	politician
elderly	person
sprightly	old man
chaotic	mess
inquiring	mind
lavish	lifestyle
sulky	teenager
affluent	neighbourhood
solemn	expression

EXERCISE 4

aggressive	behaviour
candid	opinion
impressive	home
official	warning
cultural	identity
amazing	coincidence
righteous	indignation
sterile	dressing
harsh	words

Zoggy Drives a Car on Earth

Rewrite the passage choosing the best words. Why not look in the dictionary for more choices?

Zoggy ~~wants~~ .... *(desires, craves, yearns for)* his own little car, so he ~~draws~~ .... *(sketches, designs, drafts)* one on his tablet (the latest Zen computer).

Using his exceptional alien powers, he downloads his car, gets in and embarks on his journey.

Soon he is taking a ~~drive~~ .... *(a spin, a trip, a journey, an excursion, a run)* down the motorway.

Though he hasn't ~~driven~~ .... *(operated, handled, steered, manoeuvred, controlled)* a car before, he ~~tries~~ .... *(attempts, endeavours, undertakes, strives, aims)* to drive safely.

He ~~drives~~ .... *(steers, travels)*, along the road at a very fast speed, ~~taking no notice of~~ .... *(oblivious to, ignoring, disregarding, discounting, overlooking, paying no attention to)* speed restrictions.

TAKE CARE! BE VIGILANT.
STAY ALERT. PAY ATTENTION ZOGGY!

What is that blue flashing light? Oh no! The traffic police are ~~approaching~~ .... (advancing, catching up, coming near).

Zoggy does not ~~have~~ .... (possess, hold) a driving license. He doesn't have his car taxed or insured. Will he get away with a caution for his first offence? Will he go to earth prison?

Zoggy is not keen on spying on an earth prison, so he ~~uses~~ .... (practises, applies, utilizes) his special alien powers to make himself invisible.

The police are ~~confused~~ .... (puzzled, perplexed, baffled, mystified, bewildered) that an empty car is parked on the motorway. They make arrangements to have it towed away.

Zoggy ~~starts~~ .... (commences, sets off, begins) to walk home to the safety of his space zennel.

It is nearly time to fly back to Zen, so he starts to pack his notebook full of observations in his zennel and prepares for take off. Will he be safe in space?

Rewrite the story and make it more interesting. Choose from the words in the brackets or using a thesaurus to find your own interesting vocabulary.

Some adjectives sound right with a particular noun. Match these adjectives to the most suitable noun.

EXERCISE 5

sumptuous	woman
generous	provision
abundant	stance
furtive	cloud
great	remark
threatening	tone
vivid	feast
brutal	achievement
acute	water
insulting	portion
slender	colour
tranquil	talent
exceptional	poverty
disdainful	glance
meagre	wage

EXERCISE 6

vulnerable	lifestyle
sharp	tactics
sneaky	corner
prosperous	food
secluded	pet
disdainful	child
delectable	attachment
devoted	hunt
close	smell
relentless	glance
appetising	tone
plentiful	supply
luxurious	hysteria
mass	businessman

ANSWERS   *Did you get them right?*

EXERCISE 5

sumptuous	feast
generous	portion
abundant	provision
furtive	stance
great	achievement
threatening	cloud
vivid	colour
brutal	tone
acute	poverty
insulting	remark
slender	woman
tranquil	water
exceptional	talent
disdainful	glance
meagre	wage

EXERCISE 6

vulnerable	child
sharp	tone
sneaky	tactics
prosperous	businessman
secluded	corner
disdainful	glance
delectable	food
devoted	pet
close	attachment
relentless	hunt
appetising	smell
plentiful	supply
luxurious	lifestyle
mass	hysteria

Zoggy's Big Night Out

Replace the underlined word with a similar word.

First, he sees a **grand** building with a neon sign flashing on and off above the door - 'The Royal Theatre.' There is a show on tonight starting at 7.30pm. It is **a popular** musical starring some **well-known** celebrities.

Zoggy is eagerly **anticipating** the show.

He tags on the end of the queue of earth people, but he is not sufficiently **tall** to reach up to the window of the ticket kiosk (which is just as well as he doesn't possess earth money).

Now he **clambers up** the stairs, swept along in the **immense crowd** of theatre goers, dodging the officials on the door that are checking tickets.

Soon, he **gains access** to a huge darkened hall, filled with rows of plush red velvet chairs and perches on the front row of the circle, **surveying** the scene around him. **A huge** red curtain conceals the stage; musicians play harmoniously on strange instruments.

Zoggy **leans** over the balcony precariously, to the horror of the elderly lady in the next seat. It is a big drop and he starts to feel a bit dizzy. He **scans** his programme, **savouring** his popcorn (which he found laying on the stairs as he made his way up).

The auditorium is **packed**, the theatre-goers chat together **exuberantly** and Zoggy feels a buzz of excitement.

After a few minutes, an announcement is made to **turn off** all mobile phones, so Zoggy checks his computer is on 'sleep mode' and **reclines** back in his chair, not knowing what to expect.

To his delight, the curtain **ascends** and the entertainment **begins**. The actors and actresses **gather** on the stage, **wearing** flamboyant costumes in bright colours. They start to sing and dance.

Zoggy likes the rhythm. He **delights in** the beat, but it makes him feel like joining in.
He feels an urge to tap his metal toes and jig his metal body around, so he **moves** into the aisle to dance.

"Please sit down. You are creating a **disturbance**," demands the elderly lady.
"Yes, please sit down," **scold** other members of the audience angrily.

In an instant, a hand **comes down** on Zoggy's metal body and it marches him back to his seat with a warning.
"Sit down, or you will be escorted out," **reprimands** the usher sternly.

Zoggy fidgets in his seat. He finds it **difficult** to sit still because he doesn't understand the story and he is **aware** that the lady next to him is scowling in his direction.

Fortunately for Zoggy, the interval comes quickly. The alien **stares** curiously at his surroundings. Why are people **getting up** in the middle of the performance? He joins another queue. It is long and he wonders whether he will still be queuing when the performance starts again. He **pushes himself** to the front of the queue.

Zoggy reaches out to take a share of the food but the usherette states sternly,

"No money, no ice cream."

"Please...?" Zoggy whimpers, looking pleadingly at her. The tub of ice cream is thrust at him.

"Take it, but don't breath a word to anyone, or I will lose my position." Zoggy **takes it enthusiastically** and **swallows** it in one gulp.

Now the music starts again. Zoggy **goes back** to his seat. Everyone reluctantly stands up, so he can reach his chair which is right in the middle of a row. He **squeezes** past.

When the show starts again, the music is even louder and vibrates in his metal ears, having a hypnotising effect on him. He **hears** the beat of the drums, the **sound** of guitars and he has to stand up. He has to **wave** with his antennae; he has to jig up and down - he is rocking.

The woman beside him is furious, whilst people behind are **bellowing**, "Sit down. You're spoiling the show for others."

Next, Zoggy feels the same hand come down on his metal frame. He is being **lifted up** and up, high into the air and is thrust towards the exit, along a narrow corridor and through two heavy doors - his metal frame **discarded** in a heap on the pavement outside. Crash!

The theatre door slams shut. Crowds of pedestrians push past, pretending not to see a lost alien in trouble. Zoggy recomposes himself, stands up and continues on his way.

Read, cover and write your own version. Look up any words you don't understand in the dictionary.

HELPFUL WORDS

Replace the underlined words in the previous story with the appropriate word or phrase from the list below. Remember, it is important to use the right word in the right place.

chucked	commences	consumes	bends	enjoys
clamour	eagerly	in high spirits	rebukes	an extensive
famous	an impressive	accepts it	conscious	crammed
scrambles up	raised up	proceeds to	disruption	screaming
returns	admonishes	proceeds	lofty	scrutinizing
an acclaimed	gazes at	clothed in	challenging	gains entry
moving	descends	relishing	gesticulate	listens to
thrusts himself forward	multitude	examines	switch off	lounges
forces his way	rises	awaiting	massive	warns

ANSWERS How did you do?

grand	an impressive	moves	proceeds
a popular	an acclaimed	disturbance	disruption
well-known	famous	scold	admonishes
anticipating	awaiting	comes down	descends
tall	lofty	reprimands	rebukes
clambers up	scrambles up	difficult	challenging
immense crowd	multitude	aware	conscious
gains access	gains entry	stares	examines
surveying	scrutinizing	getting up	moving
a huge	an extensive	pushes himself	thrusts himself forward
leans	bends	takes it	accepts it
scans	gazes at	enthusiastically	eagerly
savouring	relishing	swallows	consumes
packed	crammed	goes back	returns
exuberantly	in high spirits	squeezes	forces his way
turn off	switch off	hears	listens to
reclines	lounges	sound	clamour
ascends	rises	wave	gesticulate
begins	commences	bellowing	screaming
gather	congregate	lifted up	raised up
wearing	clothed in	discarded	chucked
delights in	enjoys		

Match the verbs with a suitable adjective.

stare	violently
cough	courageously
wait	gracefully
labour/slog	ferociously
fight	longingly
devour	contemptuously
dance	patiently
swerve	greedily
sneer	tirelessly
work	earnestly
growl	disobediently
plead	sharply
look	laboriously
behave	disapprovingly
visit	frequently

Can you find meanings for these theatre words?

LEISURE	AUDIENCE	PERFORMANCE	INTERVAL	REVIEW
ENCORE	THEATRE CRITIC	ACCLAIMED	RECOMMENDED	APPLAUD
STANDING OVATION	CHEERING	AUDITORIUM	FAILED TO REACH EXPECTATION	BALCONY

Which **adjectives** describe Zoggy?

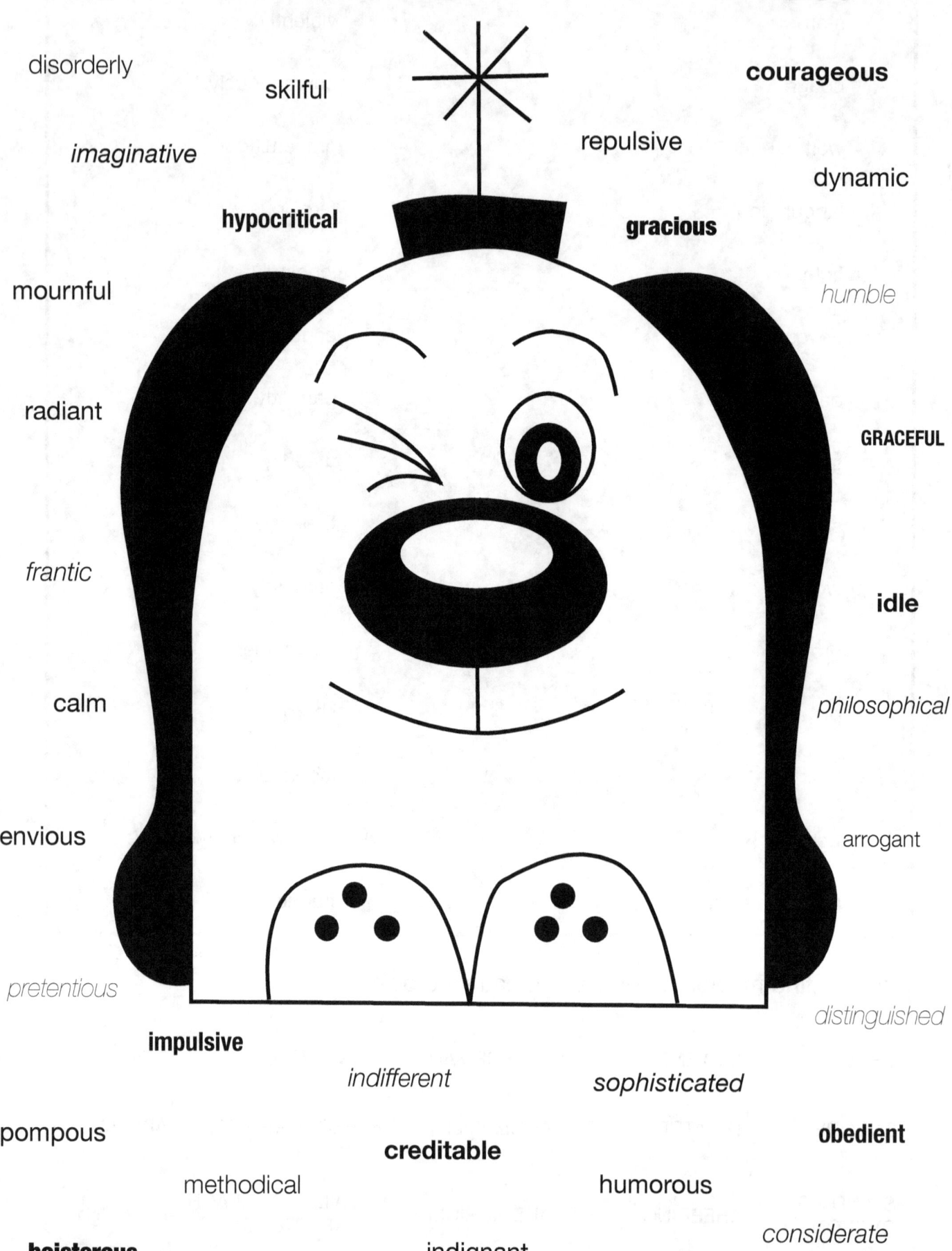

disorderly　skilful　**courageous**

imaginative　repulsive　dynamic

hypocritical　**gracious**

mournful　*humble*

radiant　GRACEFUL

frantic　**idle**

calm　*philosophical*

envious　arrogant

pretentious　*distinguished*

impulsive　*indifferent*　*sophisticated*

pompous　**creditable**　**obedient**

methodical　humorous

boisterous　indignant　*considerate*

sympathetic　obstinate

Fill in the chart:

ZOGGY WOULD LIKE TO BE:	ZOGGY WOULD NOT LIKE TO BE:
courageous	repulsive
....	....
....	....
....	....
....	....
....	....
....	....
....	....
....	....
....	....
....	....
....	....
....	....

Can you add some more words?

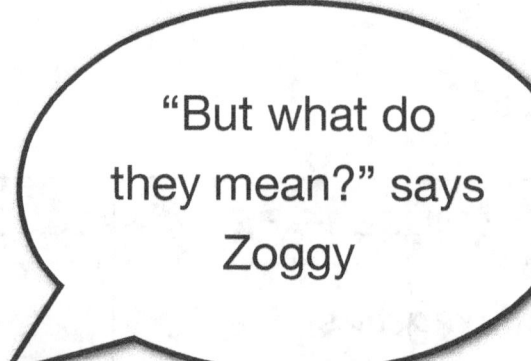

arrogant, puffed up, pretentious	pom.............................
ordinary, lovely, modest	h..................................
glowing, resplendent, shining	ra.................................
downcast, grief stricken, sombre	m.................................
active, forceful, energetic	d..................................
deceitful, deception, false, insincere	h..................................
amusing, hilarious, funny	h..................................
kind, benevolent, courteous	gr.................................
agile, elegant, smooth movements	gr.................................
desperate, distraught, frenzied	f...................................
inactive, lazy, slothful, sluggish	i...................................
celebrated, famous, acclaimed	d..................................
deformed, grotesque, ugly	rep................................
concerned, kind, obliging, unselfish	con...............................
composed, relaxed, peaceful	c...................................
jealous, resentful, begrudging	en.................................
affected, snobbish, ostentatious	pre................................
caring, compassionate	symp............................
efficient, meticulous, organised	meth............................
learned, logical, wise, stoical	phil...............................
disorganized, untidy, disruptive	dis................................
loud, noisy, unruly, disorderly	boist.............................
stubborn, dogged, immovable	obst..............................
creative, inventive, forceful	ima...............................
angry, annoyed, disgruntled	indig.............................

Zoggy tries to get fit but it all goes wrong.

Zoggy spies on the things earth, people do when they relax.

Use the Helpful Words to fill in the blanks.

"Do earthlings have time off work to do exercise?"

Zoggy .... a place with an inviting sign.

'Welcome. Join our gym. Memberships slashed to half price, this week only.'

Zoggy .... a crowd of people in a queue. Because he is so short, he has no trouble .... the reception desk (which is .... for him because he has no earth cheque book or bank card).

He .... the signs, past the changing rooms, into a room full of .... machines and he .... a buzz of excitement. Earthlings are exercising to loud rock music. He observes that humans do not choose to walk in the fresh air, but .... to walk on walking machines!

Zoggy .... the running machine and jogs up and down until he is gasping for breath; he sits .... the rowing machine and pulls with all his might; pedals .... on the cycling machine and lifts the weights until he is ....

Next, he decides to .... the swimming pool. He's never swum before, but it looks quite easy. On arriving at the poolside, he sticks one of his metal toes into the water to .... the temperature of the pool. It's warm – lovely and warm so he .... his whole body in, but he is out of his depth and he is going down, down, down under the deep water! He gasps, gurgles and ...., as he tries to breathe under the water and he thrashes about .... He has water in his eyes, his nose and his mouth! It is penetrating his metal interior and shorting out his electric circuits.

The lifeguard .... his cry for help and .... in quickly to rescue him. He grabs him, hauls him out of the water and attempts to resuscitate him, but there is .... of life (because Zoggy has automatically shut down his computer network.) The lifeguard calls 999 for an ambulance.

Before he knows it, Zoggy is .... to hospital in an ambulance. He is taken .... to the accident and emergency department - the cardio resuscitation unit. The doctor .... up to the heart monitor. It has a very strange reading.

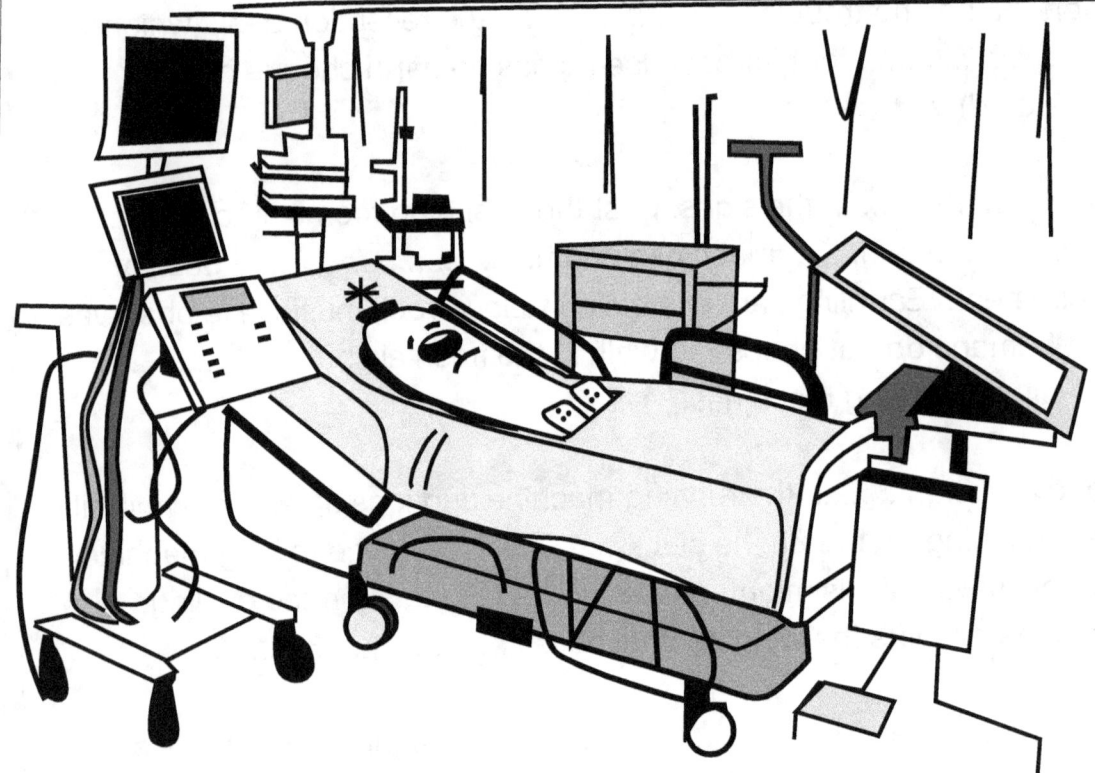

They .... his breathing, his pulse, his blood pressure and take an x ray. The readings cause .... because they are .... Meanwhile Zoggy is stirring, his computer is automatically turning on to waking mode. The doctors are ....; the patient is not responding like a normal human being. He has no pulse, because he has no blood. The high tech equipment ....
.... The doctors .... a medical emergency.

The patient is a creature that has not been previously ....; a creature that has never been seen before.

What shall we do? Who do we call? Do we call MI5? Do we send him to the Unit for Tropical Diseases? Do we alert the army? Do we phone for the police?

They radio out **RED ALERT.**

Stand by! THERE'S AN *ALIEN* INVASION!

Zoggy is coming round. His computer system is fully working and he is becoming conscious. What's that strong smell of disinfectant he thinks to himself? Where is he? He is being wheeled on a trolley to a secure room and the door is being firmly ....

He ....!

There is no time to be lost. Summoning all his strength together and every bit of brainpower, he focuses on his alien spacecraft - his zennel. He pictures it in his mind and sees himself getting into it. What's that? Some men are .... They are .... round the door, peering in, their eyes bulging.

ZOOM! In an agonising moment, his special alien powers .... him out of the hospital - back, back, back to his holiday home, where he .... the rest of his possessions, especially the notebook, where he has written his observations of earth, used on his spying missions. In a second, he has finished packing and loaded everything into his spacecraft.

Then **ZOOOOOOOOOOM UP, UP, UP!**

The men in the military uniforms, followed by the police, doctors, personnel from MI5 and four government officials, throw open the door in anticipation..... but HE'S GONE!

They .... the room, but there is no sign of him.

He has vanished into thin air.

"............................", comments one of the doctors. "If I had not seen it with my own eyes, I would never have .... it."

The men in military uniform, the police, MI5 and government officials look .... at the doctors.

"We have the X ray pictures," insist the third doctor, ... the photographs into the hands of the official men.

"Very strange indeed," they remark incredulously.

REPORT: AUGUST 14TH 2030

POSSIBLE ALIEN INVASION

EVIDENCE: INCONCLUSIVE

HELPFUL WORDS

Replace the missing words in the previous story with the appropriate word or phrase from the list below. Remember, it is important to use the right word in the right place.

examine	encountered	extraordinary	enters	desperately
mounts	follows	prefer	baffled	assembles
panics	believed	accompanies	impressive	experiences
astride	bleeps	declare	search	splutters
investigate	thrusting	blue in the face	hears	persistently
concern	directly	wires him	approaching	transport
bolted	peeping	dives	no sign	dodging
convenient	exhausted	plunges	frantically	quickly
Fascinating	conscious	test	sceptically	rushed

ANSWERS *How did you do?* *These are only suggestions.*

1. enters
2. accompanies
3. dodging
4. convenient
5. follows
6. impressive
7. experiences
8. prefer
9. mounts
10. astride
11. frantically
12. blue in the face / exhausted
13. examine
14. test
15. plunges
16. splutters
17. desperately
18. hears
19. dives
20. no sign
21. rushed
22. directly
23. wires him
24. investigate
25. concern
26. extraordinary
27. baffled
28. bleeps
29. persistently
30. declare
31. encountered
32. bolted
33. panics
34. approaching
35. peeping
36. transport
37. quickly
38. assembles
39. search
40. Fascinating
41. believed
42. sceptically
43. thrusting

Zoggy's **WAR** on *WORDS*.

Make up Zoggy's thesaurus. Add to the ideas. Use a dictionary to help you.

It is the start (................) of a new day. Zoggy dozes, slumbers, feels drowsy (................).

As he is still tired, he feels sluggish, lethargic, inactive (................)

He relaxes. His bacon fries, sizzles, crackles (................)

It is a fine, beautiful (................) day.

The sun shines brightly, is hot, boiling (................).

Zoggy gazes, observes (................) the views of earth.

Butterflies fly by, flutter (................).

Birds swoop, soar, sail by (................)

Trees rustle (................) in the breeze.

Worms slither (................).

Bees buzz (................).

The sweet smell, fragrance (................) of flowers reaches his nose.

A dog barks (................).

A wasp attacks (................).

A helicopter drones (................).

A night owl howls (................).

A fox barks (................).

Zoggy explores (................) the local area.

Zoggy's throat is sore, painful, agonising, intense, acute (................).

He has succumbed to, gone down with, caught (................) an earth cold.

He feels distressed, disgruntled, dismayed (................).

His new house looks (................) good.

He has got (................) useful furniture.

He sees (................) his neighbours.

In the afternoon, he walks (................) in the park.

"Come on in," he says (................) to his neighbour.

HARDER WORDS

The _occupant_ (...............) is an alien.

The garden is _neglected_ (...............).

He _conceals_ (...............) his spacecraft behind the hedge, so there is no evidence of an alien invasion.

You can _observe_ (...............) its silhouette in the shadows.

Zoggy _concedes, defeats, admits_ (...............) his metal legs are not made for gym equipment.

Zoggy _defends_ (...............) himself saying aliens don't need to exercise, because they automatically eject fat from their bodies.

He _stares_ (...............) in disbelief.

He looks around _cautiously_ (...............).

His computer _indicates_ (...............) that he will shut down.

On his walk, Zoggy _stumbles_ (...............) on a stone but disentangles himself.

He _confides_ (...............) in his pet mouse.

Zoggy is _reluctant_ (...............) to eat spinach even though it is a super food.

Remember a word that means the same as another is a **synonym**.

bucket → *pail*

convenient → *labour saving*

expect → *predict* → *forecast*

impressive → *dramatic*

bright → *sharp* → *astute*

awful → *deplorable*

Remember **antonym** is a word that means the opposite.

swift → *slow*

pessimistic → *optimistic*

IN THE SHOP:
- jostle
- scramble
- push
- shove

IN THE CAR:
- swerve
- veer
- deviate
- turn sharply

FEEL CALM:
- cool
- dispassionate
- indifferent
- philosophical

FEEL CAUTIOUS:
- ....
- ....
- ....

FEEL SUPERIOR:
- ....
- ....
- ....

FEEL INFERIOR:
- ....
- ....
- ....

ASCEND:
- ....
- ....
- ....

DESCEND:
- ....
- ....
- ....

www.ingramcontent.com/pod-product-compliance
Lightning Source LLC
Chambersburg PA
CBHW050715090526
44587CB00019B/3390